EMMANUEL JOSEPH

The Healing Edifice, How Architecture and Mythology Influence Modern Medicine

Copyright © 2025 by Emmanuel Joseph

All rights reserved. No part of this publication may be reproduced, stored or transmitted in any form or by any means, electronic, mechanical, photocopying, recording, scanning, or otherwise without written permission from the publisher. It is illegal to copy this book, post it to a website, or distribute it by any other means without permission.

First edition

This book was professionally typeset on Reedsy.
Find out more at reedsy.com

Contents

1. Chapter 1: The Foundations of Healing Spaces — 1
2. Chapter 2: Mythological Influence on Healing Practices — 3
3. Chapter 3: The Role of Sacred Geometry in Healing Spaces — 5
4. Chapter 4: The Healing Power of Light and Color — 7
5. Chapter 5: The Influence of Nature in Healing Spaces — 9
6. Chapter 6: The Role of Sound in Healing — 11
7. Chapter 7: The Impact of Space and Layout on Healing — 13
8. Chapter 8: The Influence of Cultural and Religious Beliefs — 15
9. Chapter 9: The Role of Technology in Modern Healing Spaces — 17
10. Chapter 10: The Impact of Community and Social Support — 19
11. Chapter 11: The Future of Healing Spaces — 21
12. Chapter 12: Conclusion: The Power of Healing Spaces — 23
13. Chapter 13: The Role of Art in Healing Spaces — 25
14. Chapter 14: Healing Spaces for Mental Health — 27
15. Chapter 15: Integrating Wellness and Prevention in... — 29

1

Chapter 1: The Foundations of Healing Spaces

Architectural design has been integral to healing since ancient times. The first healing spaces were temples and sanctuaries dedicated to gods of health and medicine. For example, the Greeks built the Asclepieia, healing temples dedicated to Asclepius, the god of medicine. These structures were meticulously designed to promote physical and spiritual healing, with tranquil surroundings and open courtyards that allowed patients to connect with nature.

In modern times, the principles of these ancient healing spaces are still relevant. Hospitals and healthcare facilities are designed with patient well-being in mind, incorporating natural light, green spaces, and calming colors to create a healing environment. The layout of these spaces is also crucial, with easy navigation and comfortable waiting areas to reduce stress and anxiety for patients and their families.

Furthermore, the concept of biophilic design, which emphasizes the connection between humans and nature, has gained traction in healthcare architecture. Studies have shown that exposure to natural elements can reduce stress, improve mood, and accelerate healing. As a result, many healthcare facilities now incorporate gardens, indoor plants, and water features into their design.

THE HEALING EDIFICE, HOW ARCHITECTURE AND MYTHOLOGY INFLUENCE MODERN MEDICINE

The evolution of healing spaces reflects a growing understanding of the holistic nature of health. By combining architectural design with principles of well-being, modern healthcare facilities can create environments that promote healing on multiple levels, from the physical to the emotional and spiritual.

2

Chapter 2: Mythological Influence on Healing Practices

Mythology has played a significant role in shaping medical practices throughout history. Ancient civilizations often attributed disease and healing to the actions of gods and goddesses. For example, the Egyptians believed that the god Thoth was responsible for healing and that invoking his name could cure ailments. Similarly, the Greeks called upon Asclepius and his daughters, Hygieia and Panacea, for healing and protection.

These mythological beliefs influenced the development of early medical practices and rituals. In many cultures, healers were also priests or shamans who performed ceremonies and offered sacrifices to appease the gods. The use of herbs, charms, and incantations in healing was common, as these were believed to harness the power of the divine.

In modern medicine, the influence of mythology can still be seen, albeit in more symbolic forms. The rod of Asclepius, a serpent-entwined staff, remains a symbol of medicine and healing. This enduring symbol serves as a reminder of the deep connection between myth, healing, and the human experience.

Moreover, the psychological impact of mythological symbols and rituals cannot be underestimated. The belief in a higher power or the use of familiar symbols can provide comfort and reassurance to patients, enhancing their overall well-being. By acknowledging the role of mythology in healing, modern medicine can tap into the power of these ancient practices to support the healing process.

3

Chapter 3: The Role of Sacred Geometry in Healing Spaces

Sacred geometry has been used in architectural design for centuries to create harmonious and balanced spaces. The principles of sacred geometry, which include the use of specific shapes, proportions, and patterns, are believed to have a positive impact on physical and emotional well-being. Ancient civilizations, such as the Egyptians and Greeks, used sacred geometry in the construction of temples and healing centers, believing that these designs could enhance the flow of energy and promote healing.

In modern healthcare architecture, the principles of sacred geometry are still relevant. Designers often use geometric patterns and proportions to create spaces that feel balanced and harmonious. This can include the use of the golden ratio, a mathematical proportion found in nature, which is believed to create a sense of beauty and order.

The use of sacred geometry in healing spaces can also have a psychological impact on patients. The symmetry and balance of geometric designs can create a sense of calm and stability, which can be particularly beneficial for patients experiencing anxiety or stress. By incorporating sacred geometry into the design of healthcare facilities, architects can create environments that support the healing process on multiple levels.

Furthermore, the use of sacred geometry in healing spaces can foster a sense of connection and meaning for patients. The knowledge that the space they are in has been designed with intention and purpose can provide comfort and reassurance, enhancing their overall sense of well-being. By blending ancient principles with modern design, architects can create healing spaces that are both aesthetically pleasing and functionally effective.

4

Chapter 4: The Healing Power of Light and Color

Light and color have long been recognized for their healing properties. In ancient times, the Egyptians used sunlight and colored gemstones in their healing practices, believing that different colors could influence the body's energy and promote healing. This practice, known as chromotherapy, has its roots in the idea that colors have specific wavelengths and frequencies that can impact our physical and emotional well-being.

Modern healthcare architecture often incorporates the principles of chromotherapy to create healing environments. Natural light is a critical component, as it has been shown to improve mood, reduce stress, and promote faster recovery in patients. Large windows, skylights, and open spaces are commonly used in healthcare facilities to maximize natural light and create a connection with the outside world.

The use of color in healthcare design is also essential. Different colors can evoke various emotional responses and influence patients' moods. For example, blue and green are often used in healthcare settings because they are calming and soothing, while warm colors like yellow and orange can create a sense of warmth and comfort. By carefully selecting colors, designers can create environments that support the healing process and enhance patient well-being.

The psychological impact of light and color cannot be overstated. A well-lit, colorful environment can create a sense of hope and positivity, which can be particularly important for patients facing challenging medical conditions. By harnessing the healing power of light and color, architects and designers can create spaces that promote health and well-being on multiple levels.

5

Chapter 5: The Influence of Nature in Healing Spaces

Nature has a profound impact on our health and well-being, and this connection has been recognized for centuries. Ancient healing centers often included gardens and natural landscapes, providing patients with access to fresh air and natural surroundings. The Greeks and Romans, for example, built healing temples and baths in natural settings, believing that nature played a crucial role in the healing process.

In modern healthcare architecture, the integration of nature into healing spaces is a growing trend. The concept of biophilic design emphasizes the importance of connecting with nature to promote health and well-being. This can include the use of natural materials, indoor plants, and views of nature to create a calming and restorative environment.

Research has shown that exposure to nature can reduce stress, lower blood pressure, and improve overall mood. Healthcare facilities that incorporate natural elements, such as gardens, water features, and green walls, provide patients with a sense of tranquility and connection to the natural world. These elements can create a more welcoming and healing environment, enhancing the overall patient experience.

The use of nature in healing spaces also extends to outdoor areas. Healing gardens and outdoor spaces provide patients with opportunities for relaxation and reflection, promoting physical and emotional well-being. By incorporating nature into the design of healthcare facilities, architects can create environments that support the healing process and improve patient outcomes.

6

Chapter 6: The Role of Sound in Healing

Sound has been used as a healing tool for centuries, with ancient civilizations recognizing its ability to influence the mind and body. The Greeks, for example, used music and chanting in their healing practices, believing that specific sounds could promote relaxation and healing. This practice, known as sound therapy, is based on the idea that sound vibrations can affect our physical and emotional well-being.

In modern healthcare design, the principles of sound therapy are often incorporated to create healing environments. Soft, soothing music can be played in waiting areas and patient rooms to reduce stress and anxiety. The use of sound-absorbing materials and acoustic design can also help create a quieter and more peaceful environment, which can be beneficial for patients and staff.

The psychological impact of sound cannot be underestimated. A calm and quiet environment can create a sense of tranquility and relaxation, which can be particularly important for patients recovering from surgery or facing serious medical conditions. By incorporating sound therapy principles into the design of healthcare facilities, architects can create spaces that support the healing process on multiple levels.

Furthermore, the use of natural sounds, such as birdsong or flowing water, can enhance the connection to nature and create a more soothing environment. These sounds can be integrated into the design of indoor and outdoor spaces, providing patients with a sense of comfort and relaxation. By harnessing the healing power of sound, architects and designers can create environments that promote health and well-being.

7

Chapter 7: The Impact of Space and Layout on Healing

The layout and organization of healthcare spaces play a crucial role in the healing process. Ancient healing centers, such as the Roman baths, were designed with specific areas for different healing activities, creating a sense of order and purpose. This approach to space and layout is still relevant in modern healthcare architecture, where thoughtful design can enhance the patient experience and support the healing process.

One key aspect of healthcare design is the flow of space. Efficient and intuitive layouts can reduce stress for patients and staff, improving overall satisfaction and outcomes. This can include clear signage, logical pathways, and easily accessible facilities to ensure that patients can navigate the space with ease.

The use of zones and dedicated areas for different functions is also important in healthcare design. For example, separating noisy and quiet areas can create a more peaceful environment for patients. Waiting areas, treatment rooms, and staff spaces should be thoughtfully designed to support the specific needs of each function, creating a harmonious and efficient environment.

The psychological impact of space and layout cannot be overstated. A well-designed healthcare facility can create a sense of calm and order, which can be particularly important for patients experiencing stress or anxiety. By incorporating principles of spatial organization and thoughtful layout into the design of healthcare facilities, architects can create environments that support the healing process and enhance patient well-being.

8

Chapter 8: The Influence of Cultural and Religious Beliefs

Cultural and religious beliefs have a significant impact on healing practices and the design of healing spaces. Different cultures have unique approaches to medicine and healing, often rooted in their spiritual and religious traditions. For example, traditional Chinese medicine incorporates concepts such as Qi, Yin and Yang, and the Five Elements, which are deeply connected to Chinese philosophy and spirituality.

In healthcare architecture, it is essential to consider the cultural and religious needs of patients. This can include the design of spaces that accommodate specific religious practices, such as prayer rooms or meditation areas. Additionally, the use of culturally significant symbols, colors, and materials can create a sense of familiarity and comfort for patients from diverse backgrounds.

Respecting and incorporating cultural and religious beliefs in healthcare design can enhance the patient experience and support the healing process. For example, some cultures believe in the healing power of water, which can be incorporated into the design through features such as fountains or water gardens. Others may emphasize the importance of natural light and ventilation, which can be achieved through open windows and skylights.

By acknowledging and honoring cultural and religious beliefs, healthcare architects can create spaces that are not only functional but also meaningful and supportive for patients from all walks of life. This holistic approach to healthcare design recognizes the importance of addressing the physical, emotional, and spiritual needs of patients.

9

Chapter 9: The Role of Technology in Modern Healing Spaces

The rapid advancement of technology has transformed the design and functionality of healthcare spaces. Modern hospitals and clinics are equipped with cutting-edge medical technologies that enhance patient care and improve outcomes. However, the integration of technology into healing spaces must be carefully managed to ensure that it supports, rather than detracts from, the healing environment.

One key aspect of technology in healthcare design is the use of smart systems that streamline operations and improve efficiency. For example, electronic health records (EHR) systems allow for seamless communication and coordination among healthcare providers, reducing the risk of errors and improving patient care. Additionally, smart building technologies, such as automated lighting and climate control, can create a more comfortable and energy-efficient environment.

Telemedicine is another technological advancement that has reshaped healthcare spaces. The ability to conduct virtual consultations and remote monitoring has expanded access to care and allowed patients to receive medical attention from the comfort of their homes. Healthcare facilities must be designed to accommodate these technologies, with dedicated spaces for telemedicine consultations and the necessary infrastructure to support high-speed internet and secure data transmission.

The use of technology in healthcare design also extends to patient engagement and experience. Interactive displays, mobile apps, and wearable devices can empower patients to take an active role in their care, providing them with information, reminders, and support. By incorporating technology into the design of healing spaces, architects can create environments that are both innovative and patient-centered.

10

Chapter 10: The Impact of Community and Social Support

The role of community and social support in the healing process cannot be overstated. Humans are social beings, and the presence of family, friends, and a supportive community can have a profound impact on patient well-being. In ancient times, healing centers often served as communal spaces where individuals could gather, share experiences, and support one another.

Modern healthcare design recognizes the importance of social support and community engagement. Hospitals and clinics are increasingly incorporating spaces for family members and caregivers, such as comfortable waiting areas, family rooms, and communal kitchens. These spaces provide a sense of home and create opportunities for social interaction and support.

The design of healing spaces can also promote community engagement and inclusivity. For example, some healthcare facilities host community events, support groups, and wellness programs, creating a sense of belonging and fostering connections among patients, staff, and the broader community. Outdoor spaces, such as gardens and courtyards, can serve as gathering places for relaxation and socialization.

By incorporating elements that support community and social interaction, healthcare architects can create environments that enhance the healing process and improve patient outcomes. This holistic approach to design recognizes that healing is not just an individual journey but a collective experience that benefits from the support and involvement of others.

11

Chapter 11: The Future of Healing Spaces

The design of healing spaces is continually evolving, driven by advancements in technology, changes in healthcare delivery, and a growing understanding of the holistic nature of health. As we look to the future, several trends and innovations are likely to shape the next generation of healthcare facilities.

One emerging trend is the focus on sustainability and environmentally friendly design. Green building practices, such as the use of renewable energy, sustainable materials, and waste reduction strategies, are becoming increasingly important in healthcare architecture. These practices not only benefit the environment but also create healthier indoor spaces for patients and staff.

Another trend is the integration of personalized and patient-centered design. As healthcare becomes more tailored to individual needs, the design of healing spaces must also adapt. This can include customizable patient rooms, flexible treatment spaces, and the use of data-driven design to create environments that meet the specific needs of different patient populations.

The use of virtual reality (VR) and augmented reality (AR) in healthcare design is also on the rise. These technologies can be used to create immersive healing environments, provide virtual tours and wayfinding assistance, and even support medical training and education. By leveraging VR and AR, healthcare facilities can create innovative and engaging spaces that enhance the patient experience.

As we move forward, the design of healing spaces will continue to be shaped by a commitment to holistic, patient-centered care. By embracing new technologies, sustainable practices, and the principles of well-being, architects can create environments that support the healing process and improve the overall quality of care.

12

Chapter 12: Conclusion: The Power of Healing Spaces

The design of healing spaces is a powerful tool in the promotion of health and well-being. From the influence of ancient mythology and sacred geometry to the integration of modern technology and biophilic design, the principles of architecture and healing are deeply interconnected. By creating environments that support the physical, emotional, and spiritual needs of patients, healthcare architects can enhance the healing process and improve patient outcomes.

The holistic approach to healthcare design recognizes that healing is a complex and multifaceted journey. By incorporating elements such as natural light, color, sound, and nature, architects can create spaces that promote a sense of calm, comfort, and connection. Additionally, by honoring cultural and religious beliefs and fostering community support, healing spaces can provide a sense of meaning and belonging for patients and their families.

As we look to the future, the design of healing spaces will continue to evolve, driven by advancements in technology, sustainability, and patient-centered care. By embracing these innovations and building on the wisdom of the past, we can create healing environments that are not only functional but also transformative. The power of healing spaces lies in their ability to nurture and support the human spirit, creating a foundation for health and well-being that extends beyond the physical realm.

13

Chapter 13: The Role of Art in Healing Spaces

Art has been a significant part of healing spaces since ancient times. From the intricate frescoes in Egyptian tombs to the mosaics in Roman baths, art has been used to create beautiful and meaningful environments that promote healing. Art can have a profound impact on our emotions and well-being, providing comfort, inspiration, and a sense of connection.

In modern healthcare design, the integration of art is becoming increasingly important. Hospitals and clinics often feature artwork that reflects the culture and values of the community they serve. This can include paintings, sculptures, murals, and installations that create a positive and uplifting environment for patients and staff.

The use of art in healing spaces can also have therapeutic benefits. Art therapy, which involves the use of creative expression to support mental and emotional health, is becoming more common in healthcare settings. By providing patients with opportunities to engage with art, healthcare facilities can support the healing process on multiple levels.

Moreover, the presence of art can create a more welcoming and humanized environment in healthcare facilities. By incorporating artwork that resonates with patients and their families, architects and designers can create spaces that feel less clinical and more supportive of the healing journey.

14

Chapter 14: Healing Spaces for Mental Health

Mental health is an essential aspect of overall well-being, and the design of healing spaces can play a crucial role in supporting mental health. Ancient healing centers often included areas for meditation, reflection, and spiritual practices, recognizing the importance of mental and emotional health in the healing process.

In modern healthcare design, there is a growing emphasis on creating environments that support mental health. This can include spaces that promote relaxation and stress reduction, such as quiet rooms, meditation areas, and sensory gardens. The use of natural light, calming colors, and comfortable furnishings can also create a soothing environment that supports mental well-being.

The design of mental health facilities is particularly important, as these spaces must meet the unique needs of individuals experiencing mental health challenges. This can include creating safe and secure environments, providing opportunities for social interaction, and incorporating elements that promote a sense of autonomy and control for patients.

By designing healing spaces that prioritize mental health, architects and designers can create environments that support the holistic well-being of patients. This approach recognizes that mental health is an integral part of the healing journey and that the design of healthcare spaces can play a significant role in promoting mental and emotional well-being.

15

Chapter 15: Integrating Wellness and Prevention in Healthcare Design

The focus of healthcare is increasingly shifting from treatment to prevention and wellness. Ancient healing practices often emphasized the importance of maintaining balance and harmony to prevent illness, and this holistic approach is becoming more relevant in modern healthcare design.

Healthcare facilities are now being designed to support not only the treatment of illness but also the promotion of overall health and wellness. This can include incorporating fitness and wellness centers, offering programs and services that support healthy lifestyles, and creating environments that encourage physical activity and healthy behaviors.

The design of wellness spaces can include elements such as exercise rooms, yoga studios, and outdoor walking paths. These spaces provide patients, staff, and the community with opportunities to engage in physical activity and promote their overall health. Additionally, wellness programs, such as nutrition counseling, stress management workshops, and mindfulness classes, can be integrated into the design of healthcare facilities to support preventive health.

By focusing on wellness and prevention, healthcare architects can create spaces that promote a holistic approach to health. This approach recognizes that maintaining health and well-being is an ongoing journey and that the design of healthcare spaces can play a crucial role in supporting this journey.

Book Description

"The Healing Edifice: How Architecture and Mythology Influence Modern Medicine" delves into the fascinating intersection of architecture, mythology, and modern healthcare design. This thought-provoking book explores how ancient principles and practices have shaped contemporary healing spaces and influenced the way we approach health and well-being.

From the sacred geometry of ancient temples to the biophilic design of modern hospitals, each chapter uncovers the profound impact of architectural design on the healing process. The book also highlights the enduring influence of mythology on medical practices, revealing how symbols, rituals, and beliefs continue to shape our understanding of health and healing.

Through a holistic lens, "The Healing Edifice" examines the role of light, color, nature, sound, and art in creating environments that support physical, emotional, and spiritual well-being. It also addresses the importance of cultural and religious beliefs, community support, technology, and mental health in the design of healing spaces.

As we look to the future, this book offers insights into the emerging trends and innovations that will shape the next generation of healthcare facilities. With a focus on sustainability, patient-centered design, and preventive health, "The Healing Edifice" provides a comprehensive and inspiring vision for the future of healing spaces.

Whether you are an architect, healthcare professional, or simply interested in the connection between environment and well-being, "The Healing Edifice" offers a rich and engaging exploration of how architecture and mythology influence modern medicine.

www.ingramcontent.com/pod-product-compliance
Lightning Source LLC
LaVergne TN
LVHW020739090526
838202LV00057BA/6123